GLA

Ghost

Prepare to be frightened by these terrifying tales from
around Glasgow

By

Gregor Stewart

BRADWELL
BOOKS

Published by Bradwell Books
9 Orgreave Close Sheffield S13 9NP
Email: books@bradwellbooks.co.uk

British Library Cataloguing in Publication Data: a catalogue
record for this book is available from the British Library.
1st Edition

ISBN: 9781910551745

Design & Typesetting by: JenksDesign

Photograph Credits: iStock, the author and credited
individually

Print: Gomer Press, Llandysul, Ceredigion SA44 4JL

CONTENTS

INTRODUCTION TO GLASGOW

When people think of Glasgow today, many will picture the strong industrial links or its football teams, rather than haunted places. However, with a documented history dating back to 1119 when the Cathedral was first built, Glasgow has more than its fair share of ghostly tales.

From its humble beginnings as a small, rural settlement, Glasgow has grown to be Scotland's largest city. It was the Act of the Union in 1707, which brought together the parliaments of England and Scotland, that would result in rapid growth and fortunes for the city. The trading port of Glasgow now had access to the vast markets of the British Empire, and its location and deep-water port led it to become the main port for the Americas, primarily in sugar, tobacco and cotton. The new wealth saw large, prestigious houses being built for the merchants and industrialisation brought further fortunes, but it wasn't to last. The Great Depression after the First World War hit Glasgow hard due to the loss of world trade leading to massive urban decay that continued until the 1950's, when the city re-established itself as a financial and media centre.

With such a long history, of religion, fortunes, loss and regrowth, the people of Glasgow have been witness to the darker side of human life. Religion brought persecution for those with opposing beliefs, wealth brought opportunists who sought to take a share for themselves, lawfully or otherwise, creating a criminal underworld and the decline brought misery and suffering. All of these are circumstances that result in incidents from which tales of hauntings originate, and it is these stories that I have brought together for this book.

TRANSPORTATION GHOSTS

Glasgow Central Station is the largest of the city centre railway stations. When it opened in 1879 it had eight platforms, but has since grown to fifteen, and is now the busiest station in Scotland. The station is fronted by the Central Hotel, one of the most impressive hotels in the city. With its long history, rapid expansion and thousands of people walking across the platforms every day, it should not be surprising to learn that there have been several incidents resulting in the station being believed to be haunted.

View of Central station from 5th floor of Radisson SAS hotel. Creative Commons

The ghost of a woman has been witnessed in a former boiler room at the station. She is believed to be the wife of a successful businessman, who lost everything he had worked for during the

Wall Street Crash in 1929. In his desperation, there was only one way he could see to regain at least some of the money he had lost, and he is said to have murdered his wife in the boiler room so that he could claim against her life insurance. In 2013, this area was investigated by the Ghost Club, the world's oldest organisation associated with psychical research. They detected the presence of a female spirit in the room, but interestingly also felt there was a male spirit with American connections also present. Using specialist equipment, they asked a number of questions and the responses indicated that the woman was stabbed to death, and her husband was hanged for his crime. Responses from what sounded like a male voice were also picked up, and so it is possible that the couple have been reunited in death.

In another part of the station, a former grain store is avoided by staff after several saw the ghost of a tall, thin woman with long, brown hair standing staring at them from within its walls. Little is known about the identity of this woman or why she would haunt this location.

The most haunted area of the station, however, is beneath it. The site chosen for the station was the village of Grahamston, and most of the buildings were demolished to make way for the railway. Low-level platforms were constructed, below those that can be seen today, to serve the Glasgow Underground, and it is in this area that the ghost of a little girl wearing old-fashioned clothing has been seen. It is believed she is one of the former residents of Grahamston, who still wanders the long-forgotten streets that were once home.

The phantom girl is not the only spook associated with the underground, which dates back to 1896 and is classed as the third oldest underground railway in the world. The chosen route was perhaps, in hindsight, unfortunate as the workmen digging the tunnels are reported to have started to discover human remains. Before long, it was apparent they had come across one of the many plague pits in the city, where mass burials took place to dispose of the bodies in an attempt to stop the spread of the disease. The discovery left the men with an uneasy feeling, but they had no option but to work their way through the bodies.

Events in the tunnel were to become far more terrifying when the workers witnessed a ball of light rising from the remains of the

St Enoch Subway Station. Thomas Nugent

plague pit. As they watched, the light ball started to grow in size, until it filled the whole tunnel and engulfed some of the men. Those caught inside the light reported hearing loud clattering noises, similar to pots and pans being banged together, or possibly bones, and seeing the tormented faces of those long deceased swirling within the mist. It would seem that, in disturbing the long forgotten bodies, the workmen had awoken a spirit, which was named 'The Clatter' due to the noise heard inside the light. The Clatter became the most feared paranormal activity during the construction of the underground, but when the railway was opened and trains began to run, sightings ceased.

This was not, however, the end of strange activity in this section of the tunnels. In the mid-1950s, workmen carrying out routine checks spotted a small figure in the tunnel. Believing it to be a young boy who had somehow managed to find his way into the depths of the underground, they approached to take the boy to safety. As they got closer, however, they realised the figure was eating something, which they soon realised was raw meat. The boy looked at them and they saw that his face had the appearance of being half human, half animal. After fleeing the tunnel, the workmen discovered that the figure, known as The Ghoul, had in fact been seen several times throughout the history of the underground, always eating what looks like a chunk of raw meat.

Other phantoms associated with the underground include the Smiling Lady of Hillhead, who, as her name suggests, appears at Hillhead Station, and is always seen smiling towards anyone who witnesses her. In the 1970s, she was seen on two consecutive nights by maintenance staff working after the station was closed, and in the 1990s a member of staff watched as she walked confidently along the platform, singing as she went, before suddenly vanishing.

The ghost of another lady is reported at West Street Station, although this phantom, known as the Grey Lady, is rather more sombre. She is believed to be the spirit of a woman who fell from the platform in the 1920s, while holding a baby. Staff acted quickly and were able to lift the baby from the track, but were unable to save the woman from the fast-approaching train. The Grey Lady is more often heard rather than seen, with many reports of a woman crying being heard from the track area, along with footsteps walking along the empty platform.

Another ghost of West Street Station is that of Robert Cobble, an unfortunate gentleman who once enjoyed a life of luxury yet died a homeless beggar. Robert had been born into a wealthy family, but in adulthood he became quite eccentric, both in his clothing and the stories he told. He became distant from his family, but popular in the local bars where he entertained the drinkers with his tall tales. Today, it would seem clear that Robert was suffering from some form of mental illness, but such things were not as well diagnosed or treated during his life, and from the time he spent in the pubs, Robert soon became an alcoholic. Having lost all contact with his family, along with his house and belongings, Robert began to sleep in a shop doorway close to the station and it was there that he was viciously beaten one night in an unprovoked attack and left for dead. He survived, but suffered permanent injuries. Despite this, his outlook on life remained positive and he still delighted in telling his tales to anyone who would listen. In the early 1900s his body was found at the doorway to the station where he had tried to find some shelter from the cold night air. Since then, the spirit of a dishevelled man has been seen at the station entrance, sometimes said to appear shivering and even almost blue in appearance, and this figure is believed to be the ghost of Robert Cobble, remaining at the place he froze to death.

Numerous other ghostly encounters have been experienced in the underground, which cannot be put down to one specific spirit. Workmen frequently report tools going missing, only to reappear later in the exact spot they were left, or to be found in a completely different part of the underground. Strange lights are also witnessed, along with unexplained noises and disembodied voices. A cat has also been seen on one of the platforms, which may not seem odd until you learn that those who have seen it report that it disappears in front of their eyes. Potential poltergeist activity has been encountered around St Enoch Station, where it is said objects would levitate as terrified employees watched, a strange slime would ooze from the walls and there were claims of people being pushed by unseen forces.

Although not strictly speaking a ghost of the underground, a curious sight has also been witnessed just outside St George's Cross Station. The figure of a man, dressed in Victorian clothing, is seen suspended in mid-air, with his head bent to one side, leading to those who have seen him saying he looks as though he has just been hanged, although no noose or gallows is visible.

The spirits of Glasgow's travel network are not limited to just the stations and underground. In Sauchiehall Street, one of Glasgow's main shopping and business areas, tramcars used to run along the 1.5-mile stretch on a regular basis until the 1960s when they ceased to operate and the tracks were removed. That was not to be the end of the trams, though, as one is still reported to run silently up and down the street. The phantom tram is said to be driven by a seemingly emotionless driver and appears so clearly that on one occasion a member of the public, who was unaware that the tram system no longer operated, hailed the driver to stop. The driver smiled and nodded politely, before the whole vehicle slowly disappeared in a cloud of sudden mist, leaving the terrified witness questioning what he had just seen.

The Kelvin Hall. Author's collection

The Glasgow Museum of Transport, now situated at Glasgow Harbour, was originally operated from the former tram depot at Pollokshields when it was established in 1964, before moving to Kelvin Hall in 1987.

It was while the museum was based at the Kelvin Hall, a building which dates back to 1927, that the large, open spaces available were utilised and a recreation of a full scale Glasgow street, as it would have appeared in the 1930s, was built. The street scene included a cobbled road, shops, a cinema, an underground railway station and various vehicles from the time, giving visitors a real feel for typical life in Glasgow in the thirties. It seems perhaps that this was too realistic, as before long unexplained activity began to be reported. Footsteps were heard by staff and visitors on the cobbles behind them, but when they checked no one was there. The sound of someone limping, or dragging their leg, was also heard but, upon investigation, again those who had heard it found themselves alone. Night guards reported seeing strange lights floating along the street scene when the building was closed, and the sound of children laughing was heard both day and night. Shadowy figures were also seen within the shops and the cinema and some guests reported feeling someone tap them on the shoulder, but when they turned to look they discovered there were was no one behind them.

In March 2005 the Ghost Club carried out an investigation at the Museum of Transport. Having completed their initial walk round and set up some equipment, they returned to the cinema where they noted several of the spring-loaded seats were in the down

The Street Scene. Photo Courtesy of William Allan

position, as though someone was sitting on them. Some of the members reported that they had checked earlier, and all the seats were in the upright position at that time. While the entire team were in the cinema, motion sensors that had been set up on the street exhibition outside were activated on two occasions but, each time, no cause was found. Unexplained fluctuations in temperature were also registered and numerous unusual noises heard and recorded.

It is not clear why the street scene came to be so paranormally active. Some have suggested that the Kelvin Hall was used as a morgue during the blitz at the start of World War II, when the

Clydebank area of the city was targeted for two consecutive nights by over two hundred German bombers, resulting in 528 civilians being killed and tens of thousands losing their homes. It may well be that the spirits of some of those who suffered sudden death remained in the Kelvin Hall where their bodies had lain, and were attracted to the street scene as it would appear familiar to them.

THE GLENLEE TALL SHIP

A short distance from Glasgow city centre, sitting on the bank of the River Clyde, lies the Riverside Museum, the new home for Scotland's Museum of Transport and Travel, where one of the main attractions, is the Tall Ship *Glenlee*.

The three-masted barque (the name refers to the set-up of the sails) was constructed on the River Clyde at Port Glasgow. Measuring approximately 245 feet long and 38 feet wide, the *Glenlee* first set sail in 1896 as a bulk cargo carrier and, during its working life, the ship circumnavigated the world four times, including passing through the feared storms of Cape Horn some fifteen times.

In 1922 the ship was sold to the Spanish navy, where it was used for training in the use of a sailing ship until 1969, when the ship was modified further to be used as a stationary training facility. In 1981 the ship was completely de-rigged, including the removal of the masts, and moved to the Spanish port of Seville, where it was planned to be used as a floating museum. Unfortunately, that plan never came to fruition and instead the ship was left, abandoned to the elements.

In 1990, naval architect Sir John Brown discovered the ship lying in Seville. By this time, it was in such a poor state of repair that plans were already being made to scrap it. Sir John, who during his career had worked on the design of famous ships such as the

Queen Mary, *Queen Elizabeth*, the Royal Yacht *Britannia* and the *QE2*, recognised the historical importance of the *Glenlee* and set about trying to rescue it and, two years later, the Clyde Maritime Trust successfully purchased the ship. After initial work to make it seaworthy again, the *Glenlee* was towed back to Glasgow, where it underwent a six-year restoration programme. By chance, the original masts and rigging were located in Spain, and returned to Glasgow to be refitted.

The *Glenlee* – which is one of only five surviving Clyde-built sailing ships and is recognised as part of the core collection of the National Historic Fleet as being of outstanding national

The Glenlee *Tall Ship*. Author's collection

significance in terms of maritime heritage, historic associations or technical innovation – is today operated as a museum and educational facility.

During the *Glenlee*'s working life, the crew members would have lived and worked in close proximity to each other for months at a time with no opportunity to leave the ship. This, combined with the poor sanitary facilities of the time, led to disease spreading easily. Bodies of those who died on board could not be kept on board due to the increased risk of disease this would have brought, and so burial at sea was not uncommon, with the dead sailors' possessions being sold to the rest of the crew. With this in mind, along with the fact that the *Glenlee* spent most of its working life in the deadliest seas of the time, it is perhaps not surprising to learn that there are reports of strange happenings on board. The most commonly reported incidents, experienced by both staff and visitors, are sudden drops in temperature and a general feeling of being uncomfortable, and even feeling unwell, in certain areas. A shadow-like figure has been witnessed many times on the ship, and footsteps are often heard with no obvious source.

It is believed the figure seen on the ship is William Pedvin, one of the crew during a voyage that is recorded simply as 'foreign' in the ship's log. Sailing under a previous name of *Islamount*, the ship left the Port of London on 8 March 1912 at 2.30pm. Just twenty days into the journey, on 28 March, William Pedvin reported to the ship's doctor complaining of pains in his bowels. The records show he was treated 'as per the medical guide'. This guide does not specifically list bowel pain, so it is difficult to say with certainty what treatment was given, but it is fair to assume from other treatments that are detailed that it would not have been particularly pleasant! On 6 April 1912 Pedvin returned to his duties and was reported as being well, and no further record regarding his health or conduct was noted until 10 February 1913, when he was unable to perform his duties due to being under the influence of alcohol. This marked the start of a decline in his health, and by 24 February 1913 he is recorded as being admitted to the ship's medical quarters, complaining of pain in his stomach, for which he refused to take medicine.

During the following months he returned to work several times for brief spells before again having to seek medical advice for stomach pains and on 25 July 2013, when he was diagnosed with bronchitis, as well as his ongoing stomach problems. He was given a purgative pill (i.e. a laxative), a herbal remedy and a glass of 'hot grog'. He once again resumed his duties on 18 March, but just three days later he was back in the medical quarters receiving treatment. On 1 September he was moved to a room in the rear of the ship which was transformed into a makeshift hospital to treat him, while also isolating him from the rest of the crew. On 7 September he is reported as being much better and able to wash and feed himself, but, as seems to have been the case previously, this was just a temporary recovery. By 12 September the records show he was very poorly, complaining of heart pain and with his mind starting to wander, and at 6.40pm on 14 September 1913 he died at the age of just fifty-four.

The following day his body was sewn up in a heavy canvas with weights attached and, at 8am, the ship was brought to a stop. With all crew present, he was lowered on a platform to the waterline, where his body slipped off and sank into the depths of the sea. There is no doubt that, even in the harsh world of early ship voyages, William Pedvin suffered a long and unpleasant death. His belongings, including his pillow and bedding, were sold to the rest of the crew by auction, with the proceeds being given to his family when the ship docked, which may explain why his spirit is still believed to walk the decks of the ship and the makeshift hospital in which he died.

The ship was visited as part of the television show *Derek Acorah's Ghost Towns*, which aired on British television on 21 November 2006. Members of staff described some of the unexplained happenings that have occurred on the ship, including the strange noises which were first heard by contractors working on the restoration of the ship. An experience that some of the staff had found particularly frightening occurred during a tour, when the guide heard the handle to a door rattle beside her. Seeing that it was moving, as though someone was trying to open the door from the inside, she opened the door only to find there was no one there. During the show, the well-known psychic and medium, Derek Acorah, picked up on two male spirits on board. He felt one had died of a heart attack or something similar on the ship, as he felt chest pains while the energy was around him. It is possible that this was the spirit of William Pedvin who, as mentioned previously, is documented as having experienced heart pain shortly before he died. The second spirit was seen in the form of a shadow figure during their investigation, and this was thought to be the ghost of the ship's cook. Acorah was able to assure the staff that both spirits were in visitation form only, meaning they were not bound to the ship and only returned at certain times, and that neither meant any harm during their visits.

HAUNTED HOSPITALS

Like most cities, Glasgow is home to several hospitals, some of which have been in use for hundreds of years. Glasgow Royal Infirmary first opened in December 1794 and has been extended considerably since then, with the original buildings being replaced at the start of the 1900s.

With such a long history, it is perhaps not surprising to learn that there are several ghost stories connected with the hospital. The *Guardian* newspaper covered some of the tales in an article

Glasgow Royal Infirmary. Author's collection

published in 2004. This included a particularly scary encounter that a young nurse named Judith Whalley had while walking through the wards one night. She saw a ward sister walking towards her and, as they approached each other, she said, 'Good evening, Sister.' The sister did not respond and it was then Judith realised there was something particularly unusual about her, as she appeared only from her knees up. It has been suggested that this is the ghost of a former sister in the hospital and, as the building has undergone several periods of renovation where floors have been lowered and raised, she still walks on the level of the floor that existed during her life.

Another ghost who is reported to have been seen many times in the hospital is the Grey Lady. Described as wearing grey clothing, the lady is seen wandering the corridors before disappearing into one of the rooms. Whenever witnesses have gone into the room after her, they have found it to be completely empty. Ward 27 is said to be haunted by the ghost of a former patient named Archie, who has been seen leaning over dying patients, as though he is talking to them. In a more recent incident, it was claimed that a doctor received an emergency call in the hospital to notify him that a patient was suffering sudden heart failure. As he rushed along the corridor to the ward, he was somewhat surprised when a patient approached him and asked him if he knew the way out. Without stopping, the doctor pointed to the door behind him and kept running. When he reached the ward he was told that the patient had already died and, when he looked down at the body, he realised it was the same man who had asked him for directions in the corridor outside.

Glasgow's Western Infirmary. Thomas Nugent

Glasgow Western Hospital was built in 1874 as a teaching hospital following the university's move to the West End of the city. Having undergone substantial rebuilding in the 1960s and 1970s, the hospital was closed down in the autumn of 2015 and is to be redeveloped by the university.

The most famous ghost encountered in the hospital is that of Sir William Macewan, a much-respected surgeon who specialised in, among other things, brain surgery. According to the tale surrounding the haunting, Sir William was approached in the hospital by an artist who asked his help as he was suffering from severe headaches. Sir William turned the young man away and, no doubt disappointed at not being able to get help, the artist made his way out of the hospital. However, he suffered another blinding headache as he made his way down the stairs, lost his balance and fell to his death. It is said Sir William never got over the guilt of not treating the artist, and after his own death in 1924 staff started to report seeing his figure still walking in the corridors, along with the distinctive smell of cigars, which Sir William regularly smoked.

Another ghostly encounter was reported as happening in 1975 when Mary McLellan was working as a ward sister at the hospital. While preparing some equipment, she became aware of a tall, grey-haired man standing near the ward, as though watching her. He was wearing a blue dressing gown and, when she looked again, he was gone. She was unconcerned, assuming it was one of the patients and that he had returned to the ward, and she carried on with her work. Almost immediately, she was disturbed by a distressed nurse running towards her. The nurse reported that she had also seen the old gentleman, and had recognised him as a patient she had been treating, but who had died two days previously.

Stobhill Hospital, situated to the north of the city, dates back to the early 1900s and is said to be haunted by a nurse who seems to still be caring for the patients, even after her own death. On one occasion, a student nurse who was looking for someone more experienced than her to answer a question is said to have spotted a woman dressed in a nurse's uniform in the corridor in front of her, before she walked into a side ward. The student nurse followed, hoping that she would find an answer to her question, but instead she found the room empty, except for the patient. She immediately realised the patient had fallen unconscious and was in urgent need of medical assistance and called for help. The patient's life was saved due to the quick intervention of the medical staff and it would appear that the spirit of the former nurse was trying to attract attention to the seriously ill patient.

BIRKWOOD CASTLE

Despite sitting around twenty five miles from Glasgow City Centre, Birkwood Castle is often included in lists of Glasgow's most haunted places. The castle was constructed in 1860 as a family home but in 1923, it was converted into a Psychiatric Hospital for children from the surrounding area, particularly Glasgow as that has the largest population. It ceased to operate as a hospital in 2002 and quickly fell into a state of disrepair.

Over the years, several ghosts have been reported at the property, particularly the spirits of children, which is perhaps not surprising given its former use. Activity experienced has included hearing the sound of a girl both weeping and singing from empty rooms within the building, along with strange smells, the sound of children running up and down the corridors and the lights switching on and off for no reason. The ghost of a boy named Michael has been witnessed several times on the main staircase of the building, and it is believed that he fell and died on the stairs. There are also the ghosts of adults within the building, including one that is not seen, but sensed through the strong smell of cigar smoke wherever he goes. There is also the ghost of a man who is said to have been stabbed at the hospital and the phantom of Doctor Richardson, a General Practitioner who suffered a heart attack while working at the hospital. His figure is most frequently seen sitting in his former office, looking out of the large window.

Developments at Birkwood Hospital took a bizarre twist in August 2015. The property by that time had been classified within the world of the paranormal as one of the countries most haunted castles, and was in the process of being converted into a hotel and luxury flats, but it seems this did not go down well with the castle's spooks. During the night, local residents reported what they thought was an explosion coming from the direction of the castle, and it was found that a significant part of the building had collapsed. Having found no reason for this, it was widely speculated and reported in the national press that the collapse may have been caused by the castle ghosts, angry that their residence was being converted from the hospital they knew.

The old entrance to Birkwood Castle. Elliott Simpson

THE SOUTHERN NECROPOLIS

Glasgow is home to two extensive cemeteries which date back to Victorian times, both bearing the name 'Necropolis', meaning City of the Dead. It is the Southern Necropolis, located in the Gorbals area of the city, where we will find our tales of hauntings.

One of the most famous stories spiralled out of all control in the 1950s. Rumours had existed for some time that the cemetery,

Southern Necropolis Gateway. Stephen Sweeney

which is the final resting place for over 250,000 souls, was also home to a seven-foot-tall vampire with metal teeth. Children avoided the area until, in 1954, news spread that the vampire had captured two children in the Southern Necropolis and was going to eat them! Over the following nights, groups of vigilante kids faced their fears and, armed with sharp sticks and knives, patrolled the graveyard hoping to capture the beast and free the prisoners. Needless to say, no vampire was found and no children had been reported as being missing, yet the story was still carried by many national newspapers.

Another ghost of the Southern Necropolis bears some resemblance to a story from St Andrews in Fife, where a stone statue of an angel above a grave in the Eastern Cemetery is reported to have moved and her figure is seen wandering the graveyard. In the Southern Necropolis, the final resting place of John Smith, a carpet manufacturer, his wife Magdalene and their housekeeper, named Mary McNaughton, is marked with a statue of a veiled lady standing beside a broken pillar. It may seem unusual for the housekeeper to be buried in the same grave as the family she worked for; however, the reason for that probably lies in the tragic circumstances surrounding her death. On 29 October 1933, while returning home from church, Magdalene Smith and Mary McNaughton sought shelter from the heavy rain behind an umbrella. With their view obstructed, they accidentally walked straight into the path of a tramcar on Queen's Drive. Magdalene died shortly after from her injuries and Mary died around two weeks later.

According to local legend, people walking through the Southern Necropolis after dusk have witnessed the head of the veiled lady turn to stare at them as they pass. The figure of a lady dressed in white is also seen walking through the cemetery, with much speculation that this is the ghost of either Magdalene or Mary. There is, however, another possibility. In St Andrews, the stone angel is believed to be the protector of the graveyard, keeping all of the souls safe. Perhaps the statue of the veiled lady has a similar role in the Southern Necropolis, and walks the grounds looking after the many people laid to rest there.

The Veiled Lady. Photo Courtesy of M J Steel Collins

DALMARNOCK BRIDGE

A total of eight bridges cross the River Clyde to keep the city of Glasgow connected. Sadly, these essential crossing points are also utilised by some for more morbid purposes, with the Dalmarnock Bridge in particular often being used by people committing suicide.

The spirit of a young man who is believed to have taken his own life has been seen many times on the bridge. Described as being around thirty years old and wearing dark clothing, the figure is

Dalmarnock Bridge. Author's collection

solid enough to make those who see him believe they are looking at a real person. One encounter is described as having taken place when the man was spotted standing at the side of the bridge, staring over into the River Clyde below. After watching the man, the witness feared he was going to jump, and rushed forwards shouting to him to stop. Just as he reached the man, he did jump, yet there was no sound of him entering the water and when the witness looked there was no sign of him. The incident was reported to the police, but no body was ever found. Several other people have reported seeing the man standing at the side of the bridge before jumping, but claim that he vanishes before he hits the water. The identity of the man or the reasons why he took his own life remain a mystery, yet sightings of his ghost still continue to be reported and so it is hoped that one day his story will be revealed.

PHANTOMS OF THE THEATRES

Situated in a district of Glasgow known as the Merchant City, due to the area's historical connections with the wealthy merchants of the city's past, stands the Tron Theatre, a building with a long and occasionally dark history. The theatre occupies a site where the sixteenth-century Church of St Mary of Loretto and St Anne once stood. In 1592, following the Scottish Reformation, the town council ordered the church to be changed from a Catholic church to a Protestant church, named the Laigh Kirk, and the following year the steeple was added, with a spire being constructed in 1636 to make the building look more like a traditional Protestant church. It remained in use as a church until 15 February 1793. On that fateful evening, members of a secretive club known as the 'Hell Fire Club' were passing the church when they noted it was empty. No doubt fuelled by drink, they decided to test one of the beliefs held by the club, that the members could withstand the fires of hell, and they sneaked into the boiler room and added as much fuel as they could manage into the furnace. The resultant heat was so great, that the building caught fire and it was completely destroyed, with the exception of the steeple.

The church was rebuilt in 1795, but by 1800 the building was being used as a meeting place for Glasgow's newly formed police force. The Industrial Revolution of the nineteenth century changed the fortunes of the area for ever and, as the wealthy

The Tron Theatre. Author's collection

moved towards the West End of the city, more undesirable characters moved in, resulting in the area becoming referred to as 'the dark side of Glasgow'. During this time, the church building had various other uses, including providing a holding cell for criminals who had been sentenced to death. The condemned prisoners were led by a tunnel from the building to Glasgow Cross, where the executions took place, but it is reported that many suffered fatal heart attacks brought about by their fear before they even made it out of the cell. The building gradually fell into a state of disrepair until 1980, when the Glasgow Theatre club took over the building and carried out extensive restoration to create the Tron Theatre and bar.

Since then, members of staff and visitors have reported sightings of mysterious figures and other unexplained experiences. A hooded figure has been witnessed several times walking through the old bar and restaurant area. The figure could date back to the time the building was used as a church, or could be one of the condemned prisoners about to be led to meet their death, or even the executioner, preparing to do his duties. Another spirit often spotted is that of a child, who is often seen looking out of the window in the east stairway. This is believed to be the spirit of a girl named Lily, who was struck by a horse-drawn cart on the street outside. The injured child was brought into the then church for assistance, but sadly died from her injuries. Perhaps she chooses this window because it looks out over the spot where she was hit.

The building is, however, also believed to house dark spirits. One former member of staff described an incident one night while they were working at the bar. They state they heard a hissing noise from behind, yet saw that there was no one there. The sound became louder and they realised it was not a hiss, but instead the word 'No' was being said, louder and louder. They moved away to another part of the bar to try to get away from the sound, but it followed, as though it was being made just inches from their ear. Suddenly they were struck with something across the back of their knees and the noise stopped.

A shadow figure is also seen in the boiler room, an area where staff report feeling very uneasy. Another member of staff reported hearing footsteps approach from behind when they were locking up, followed by the feel of ice-cold fingers running down the back of their neck. They spun round, to find they were completely alone. The Tron Theatre was visited by psychic medium Derek Acorah, who picked up on the spirits of two males in the main theatre, one aged around thirty years old, and the other, whom he believed to be a former caretaker, aged around sixty. He also sensed the spirit of a child, aged around six years old. He did not feel these spirits meant any harm but, when he was led to the boiler room, he sensed something very dark. Describing it as a negative energy, capable of splitting itself into several entities, he expressed surprise that nothing bad had occurred in the theatre, as he thought this was some form of portal created by people who had tried dark magic in the area. He sensed a tall, bald man, who was demanding that they left before something happened, while stating that he had to stay. Perhaps this negative entity is the result of a ritual carried out by the members of the Hell Fire Club and the man was one of their spirits, who chose to remain to keep whatever they had unleashed under control. Acorah certainly felt that the portal had to be closed for the safety of those in the building, and the team carried out a ceremony to do so.

The Theatre Royal on Hope Street, which opened in 1867, is the oldest theatre in Glasgow. Originally named the Royal Colosseum and Opera House before changing to the current title in 1869, the theatre operated successfully with many large productions until the start of the First World War, when, despite difficulties that many such businesses encountered such as a shortage of performers and staff, along with the difficulties in travelling, it continued to put on regular shows to lift the spirits of the people of Glasgow.

The Theatre Royal. Author's collection

In 1957 the theatre was bought by Scottish Television (STV) and it was converted into three studios for the production of television shows. In 1974, STV moved to purpose-built studios and the theatre was sold to Scottish Opera, who set about having the building restored as a stage theatre; although now considerably extended, the theatre continues to operate to this day. During its history, the building has suffered extensive fire damage on two occasions, the first being in 1879, when the auditorium was destroyed, and again in 1969, when fire crews from the surrounding areas had to be called in to tackle the blaze.

The oldest ghost of the theatre is known to the staff as Nora and is mostly heard rather than seen. The sound of moans and sighs in the upper gallery, along with doors slamming and a general feeling of being watched, are all attributed to this spirit, who is believed to be that of a failed actress. According to the legend, Nora worked at the theatre but she had always longed to be an actress. She had asked the manager on several occasions if she could audition for roles, but the manager had always refused due to her having no experience that he knew of. Eventually her persistence paid off, and he agreed to allow her to audition. His gut instincts had, however been right, and her acting was terrible. Many other members of staff, who knew of Nora's determination, had heard about the audition and had gathered to watch, with the result that she was laughed off the stage. Heartbroken that her dreams had been shattered, and humiliated by the reaction of her colleagues, Nora took her own life. It seems her love of the theatre did not die, however, and her spirit returns to watch with a mix of sadness and no doubt jealousy as others continue to perform on the stage as she longed to do. In spirit, Nora also would appear not to have forgiven her fellow workers, with staff still being said to report an unpleasant atmosphere in this area.

Another ghost that is reported at the Theatre Royal is a fireman who tragically lost his life in the fire of 1969. The fire was discovered at around 4.30pm on Tuesday 4 November 1969, when smoke started to fill one of the STV studios while a live TV show was being broadcast. The show was quickly ended and the 370 staff were evacuated, with the television station switching to showing cartoons to maintain broadcasting. Once the fire service arrived, the scale of the fire was realised. It had started in a basement area some thirty feet below ground. Later investigation revealed the fire was most likely caused by an electrical fault and, as the basement was used to store paper files, it had grown rapidly. Fifteen fire appliances ended up attending, with approximately ninety fire officers to fight the fire. The fire appeared to have been brought under control by the evening, but it broke out again, with dense smoke flowing from the basement ventilation shafts, filling the building and forcing fire officers back. High-expansion foam was pumped into the building to starve the fire of oxygen and eventually extinguish it.

According to the fire and rescue service records, at around 12.45am on the morning of Wednesday 5 November, with the fire still burning in the basement, a search started for a missing station officer, who had entered the building two hours earlier and had not returned. Although I know his name, I will not state it out of respect for the family. It was estimated that he only had one hour of oxygen in his tank when he entered the building. The search teams are said to have fought their way through up to six feet of foam in an attempt to find their comrade, but could find no trace of him. At around 2pm, the body of the station officer was found in the basement area where the fire had started. He was submerged in around six feet of water and it was not clear whether he had drowned or suffocated.

Since the tragedy, the phantom of a man wearing a fire officer's outfit consistent with that worn in the late sixties has been witnessed throughout the theatre. He has been seen sitting in the corner of one of the rooms and particularly seems to appear to musicians, sometimes staring at them in the orchestra pit. There have also been many unexplained incidents in the basement area, such as items disappearing, including workmen's tools when they were carrying out maintenance work, and these have been attributed to the ghost of the fireman.

The Pavilion Theatre in the city's Renfield Street is also reputedly haunted by several spirits. Built in 1904, the theatre featured shows with many of the big-name talents of the day, including Charlie Chaplin, and it remains substantially unaltered from the original design. A well-known and highly regarded local comedian named Tommy Morgan drew large audiences from the 1920s until the 1950s. Although Morgan never achieved the worldwide fame that others enjoyed, he was still considered to be a comic genius and he played nineteen successive summer seasons at the Pavilion Theatre. After his premature death in 1958, his dying wish was fulfilled and his ashes were scattered from the roof of the theatre. Ever since, Tommy has been seen by many, still wandering through the backstage area of the theatre and occasionally watching rehearsals from the auditorium.

The theatre has also been subject to a number of other unexplained phenomena, including a piano in the orchestra pit being heard to play by itself and one of the seats in the stalls frequently moving to the 'down' position, despite being spring-loaded to automatically be in the upright position when not in use. The ghost of a young girl and a lady have also been seen in the theatre, although the story behind their haunting is not known.

The Citizens Theatre in the Gorbals area of the city was originally known as His Majesty's Theatre when it opened in 1878. Shortly after it opened, a rather bizarre incident occurred when a performing elephant became distressed on stage, causing a stampede and riot, which left the theatre bankrupt. It reopened as the Royal Princess's Theatre in 1880 and operated until a change in ownership in 1922, when it was leased to the Citizens Theatre Company, changing its name in 1945. The theatre is reported to be haunted by a Green Lady, a traditional Scottish ghost, often associated with sadness or loss. This is believed to be the spirit of a former front-of-house manager who, according to the legend, committed suicide by throwing herself to her death from the upper balcony of the theatre.

PROVAN HALL

The edge of a 1950s housing estate is perhaps not where you would expect to find a fifteenth-century country mansion house, but that is exactly where you will find Provan Hall, in a small park named Auchinlea Park on the edge of the Easterhouse estate. The hall actually comprises two buildings, joined by a central courtyard, and has been described by the National Trust for Scotland as 'probably the most perfect pre-reformation mansion house in Scotland'.

It is not known exactly how old Provan Hall is, although it is believed that the north range dates back to the 1460s. The hall provided a country residence for the Baillie family, who held the title of Canon of Provan. In 1599 ownership of the hall and estate passed to the Hamilton family through marriage. Successive generations carried out remodelling to the property until, in 1667, the Hamiltons had to sell the hall due to historic debts. Glasgow Town Council bought the building and retained ownership until 1767, when it was sold on. The property passed through several owners in a relatively short period of time until it was bought by Dr John Buchanan, a former ship's surgeon, in 1788. This perhaps saved the hall, as it stayed within the Buchanan family, and then the Mather family through marriage, for generations. In 1934, the last direct descendant of Dr Buchanan died with no family to pass the estate onto, and so it was put up for sale again. A collective group of interested parties, private subscribers and the National Trust purchased the property, which was renovated prior to being passed to the sole ownership of the National Trust for Scotland, who continue to maintain and operate it to this day.

Provan Hall has been associated with several tales of ghostly goings-on. Visitors regularly report seeing a man dressed in old-fashioned clothing standing in the newer wing of the house, known as Blochairn House. It is widely believed that this is the spirit of Reston Mather, the last private owner of Provan Hall, whose sudden death left the building without an heir and resulted in it leaving the ownership of the family. The ghost of Reston Mather is also associated with numerous inexplicable noises coming from empty areas of the building, such as furniture being moved, particularly in the dining hall. Staff who have heard these noises are reported to have said they thought the building had been broken into yet, when they investigated, they found that no one else was there. Phantom footsteps are also heard frequently throughout the house.

The older part of the building is reputedly haunted by the ghost of a mother and her young child, who were murdered in the main bedroom. The incident is said to have happened over two hundred years ago, when a soldier who was staying at the house left his wife there for protection while he went on overseas duties. It was four years later when he finally returned, to find his wife had a daughter who was only two years of age. Realising that the young girl could not possibly be his daughter, in a fit of rage the soldier murdered his wife and the child. Ever since, the room has always felt cold and the figure of a frightened-looking woman has been seen. Some visitors have reported feeling an oppressive sensation in the room, while others are overcome with sadness and have to leave.

The courtyard between the two buildings is not without its own strange activities, with visitors reporting feeling as though they are being followed, hearing footsteps and even, on some occasions, being tapped on the shoulder, only to find when they turn around that there is no one behind them.

Provan Hall. G Laird

THE PEARCE INSTITUTE

It would be easy to mistake this impressive building situated at Govan Cross for a grand townhouse, but in fact the Pearce Institute was constructed as a community centre to provide facilities and activities for the people of Govan. The building opened in 1906 and was funded by Lady Dinah Pearce in memory of her late husband, Sir William Pearce, a prominent businessman who made his fortune through shipping and shipbuilding. The institute has remained in use ever since, always adapting to meet the changing needs of the local community and, when it faced a

The Pearce Institute. Author's collection

recent risk of closure, the support of the community ensured its survival.

For some reason, the building seems to be very active with paranormal activity, making it a favourite for ghost-hunting events. The most commonly seen ghost is that of a woman wearing what are described as fine, old-fashioned clothes. This phantom has been witnessed walking through the foyer area of the institute and also standing on a balcony overlooking one of the halls. A likeness has been noted between the spook and an old photograph of Lady Dinah Pearce, leading many to believe that the ghost is indeed that of Lady Pearce, still watching over the activities taking place and, no doubt, taking some satisfaction in seeing that the building remains in use as she originally intended. Even at times when she is not seen, her presence is felt watching visitors and staff, although all who have experienced this report that they in no way feel threatened and that the spirit is friendly.

The ghost of an elderly man wearing a long, brown coat and a quite distinctive hat has also been seen walking through the halls. The story behind this spook is not known, although again he is not considered to be threatening. The same cannot be said for a presence that is believed to remain in some areas of the building, predominantly in the basement areas, which include the boiler room and a shooting range that extends below the neighbouring graveyard. Although it is never seen, staff have reported feeling a negative energy in these areas as well as occasionally in the bell tower and the attic, leading many to believe that an evil entity also lurks within the walls of the institute.

Other unexplained activities which are often reported by both staff and visitors include taps switching on and being found to be jammed, lights turning on and off on their own, and doors opening and closing. A former caretaker is said to have had a particularly unnerving experience one night when, having completed his walk round the building to check that it was empty and secure, he suddenly heard the unmistakable sound of the organ playing from the hall. This left the caretaker terrified as not only was he alone in the building, but he knew that the organ had been decommissioned and could not be played. He is reported to have fled the building, never to return.

POLLOK ESTATE
AND HOUSE

Pollok House sits in a large country park close to the centre of Glasgow, offering a tranquil retreat from the busy city life. The estate became the ancestral home of the Maxwell family in the thirteenth century, although the present house was not constructed until 1752, with the wings being added in 1890. The property remained the home of the Maxwells until 1966, when it was gifted to Glasgow City Council, and it is now operated and maintained by the National Trust for Scotland.

In the seventeenth century the estate was at the centre of a notorious but substantially forgotten case of witchcraft, with possible connections to the famous witch trials of Salem in the United States of America. In 1677, a somewhat mysterious young lady named Janet Douglas arrived in the area. Nothing was known about where Janet had come from and, as she was mute, she could not easily communicate to tell her story. She got to know the daughters of Sir George Maxwell, the Laird of Pollok Castle, the tower house that stood in the estate prior to the current house being built. Janet learned that Sir Maxwell had recently fallen seriously unwell with an unexplained illness causing excruciating pain in his sides. Janet indicated to the laird's daughters that she felt that a woman had bewitched their father and she subsequently identified the lady in question in a crowd. Around the same time, Janet miraculously regained her ability to talk and she wasted no

Pollok House. Leslie Barrie

time in accusing five local women, a young man and a twelve-year-old girl of making a pact with the devil and inflicting the illness on the laird.

In the investigation that followed, three effigies of the laird with pins stuck in his sides were found under the guidance of Janet and, once they had been discovered, Sir Maxwell made a full recovery. Those accused by Janet were put on trial for witchcraft and, having been found guilty, they were burned at the stake, with the effigies being burned at the same time. Only the life of the twelve-year-old girl was spared. Janet was employed as a servant at Pollok before moving to Edinburgh, where she gained a reputation as a witch hunter. In such superstitious times, it was, however, not long before suspicion started to fall upon Janet herself about her apparent knowledge of the art of black magic and involvement in the sorry events that had taken place at Pollok Estate. Janet was put on trial, but never accused directly of witchcraft, which would have almost certainly resulted in her death. Instead, she was deported from the country and, although it is not clear where she was sent to, it is highly likely her final destination would be New England in America. Just a few years later, tales of witchcraft struck the small town of Salem, and the trials ensued, leaving some to speculate that Janet may have taken her stories of deals with the devil to America with her.

A section of the estate is known as Witches Wood, and there is a local belief that you can place a curse on someone who has wronged you by going to this area and leaving a message tied to the trees. People who pass through report there being an uneasy atmosphere, with some experiencing strange noises or being overcome with fear, leading it to be considered to hold a negative energy, perhaps even the spirits of those that were accused of witchcraft.

Pollok House itself is associated with many tales of unexplained happenings, including items going missing or being moved, strange noises and a shadowy figure being seen on the staircase. It has been reported that, after the house has been closed to tourists, staff have experienced poltergeist activity, such as items being thrown and people being pushed while walking down the stairs. Who, or what, might be responsible for these experiences remains unknown, although it is inevitable that the finger of blame is once again pointed towards the property's history of witch trials in the seventeenth century. This would, however, seem unlikely, given that the current house had not been constructed at that time, and the cause of the disturbances continues to intrigue ghost hunters who carry out investigations and vigils in the house.

GREENBANK HOUSE AND GARDENS

Situated just one mile away from the busy Glasgow suburb of Clarkston, the Greenbank Estate offers local residents and visitors the opportunity to feel as though they have stepped back in time as they wander through this well-preserved conservation garden with trees and shrubs, specially chosen to provide all-year-round colour.

Greenbank House. Author's collection

The estate was bought in 1763 by a local baker named Robert Allason, who had made his fortune after becoming involved in the tobacco trade. He had Greenbank House built as his family home and it remains to this day a fine example of a Georgian manor house, along with the walled gardens to provide a peaceful place to relax, which are still used by local residents and visitors for the same purpose. Allason was forced to sell the house and estate in 1784 due to financial difficulties, and over the years it changed hands several times until it was bought by William Blyth in 1961. As keen gardeners, the Blyth family set about restoring the gardens and, in 1976, they gifted the house and estate to the National Trust for Scotland, with the intention that the property was to be transformed into a gardening advice centre, offering information and inspiration to anyone from novice gardeners to professionals. Throughout the centuries, while the garden was redesigned several times, the house remained essentially untouched and today it remains much as it was when it was originally constructed.

According to the staff, there have been several reports of ghosts in both the house and the gardens. The most commonly witnessed is that of a lady wearing an elegant red crinoline dress, the style which held the dress out in a bell-like appearance and which was popular in the nineteenth century. This spirit is mainly seen standing in the dining room and although nothing is known about who she is or why she haunts the building, she has sufficiently spooked visitors that they have refused to continue with the tour and left the house.

The ghost of a young girl has also been reported in the wooded area of the garden. Wearing what is described as old-fashioned clothing, the youngster is seen skipping between the trees close to the stream, before suddenly vanishing. This is believed to be the spirit of a girl who was struck by a cart in the courtyard of the property and, sadly, died of her injuries. It would seem that she enjoyed the estate gardens so much that after her sudden and tragic death, she decided to remain. A phantom girl has also been seen in the Lodge House on the estate, although it is not clear whether this is the same ghost. The head gardener, who resides at the Lodge, reported that one morning as he came down the stairs, he saw the girl walk in through the front door and towards the kitchen, before disappearing at the bottom of the stairs. This is believed to have been the route that originally led to the kitchen before the property was remodelled, and it was concluded that the spirit was still following the layout she was familiar with, which would indicate she is a residual energy, which is one with no awareness of their current surroundings and most often seen carrying out activities as they would have done when they were alive.

The ghosts at the estate are not restricted to humans, with a large, black dog also witnessed close to an old stone bridge. One visitor reported seeing the dog on a regular basis, yet every time, as she approached the bridge, it simply vanished. Seemingly assuming the dog had just run away, she was not too spooked, but on one occasion she was accompanied by her husband and when she

pointed the dog out to him, he explained there was no dog there.
After a short discussion, it dawned on her that the dog may not be
of this world, hence its always disappearing, and she had to return
to the house to calm her nerves.

EERIE EDUCATION ESTABLISHMENTS

SCOTLAND STREET SCHOOL

Surrounded by decaying buildings, car parking and a modern road network, it is relatively easy to miss this important building that sits just outside the city centre. The significance of the property is not so much in its use, but due to its having being designed by Charles Rennie Mackintosh, one of the most famous architects in the country, whose unique style still influences modern designers today.

Built in 1903, the school on Scotland Street remained in constant use until 1979, when it was closed due to urban decay resulting in a significant drop in the number of students. The connection with Charles Rennie Mackintosh probably saved the building, and it was converted into a museum to allow people to see how education was delivered in the twentieth century, which offers the possibly unique experience of both former teachers and pupils providing the stories. It seems, however, that some of the long-deceased former teachers and pupils have also remained at the school.

The ghosts of two figures have been seen in the school, appearing as a shadow form, one on the first floor and one on the third floor. Staff report that when they are in the presence of one of these spirits, they feel particularly uncomfortable, although who they are or why they remain there is unknown. There are also numerous reports of unexplained noises coming from parts of the building that are empty, the sound of footsteps approaching when no one is there, items being moved or going missing and the sound of children whispering and giggling.

The Ghost Club carried out investigations at the school in both 2007 and 2008 and, on both occasions, they encountered phenomena such as the sound of doors slamming. They also experienced sudden drainage of their batteries and unexplained cold spots, and the shadow figures were seen by some of the group. The psychic mediums picked up on a number of children running up and down the corridors, which may be the cause for the sound of footsteps many have encountered. What is described as a heavy energy was also sensed, which the group felt was a teacher who had been cruel to the children at the school, and perhaps this was the shadowy figure that still makes staff feel uncomfortable in certain parts of the building. There was a general feeling that there was a lot of psychic energy in the building, with the suggestion that the ghostly encounters were happening due to the Stone Tape theory, under which there is a belief that energy from incidents in the past is absorbed by the stone and replayed later when the conditions are right, just in the way that images and sounds can be recorded on a tape, disc or hard drive for replay.

Scotland Street School. Author's collection

GLASGOW UNIVERSITY

The University of Glasgow sits in an elevated position just a short distance from the city centre. As mentioned in the introduction, the university was founded in 1451 and is the second oldest university in Scotland. With such a long history, it is difficult to imagine just how many people have passed through the university and, perhaps unsurprisingly, it seems that some still linger.

The university is home to a spirit known simply as the Grey Lady, which is possibly one of the most unusual ghosts that I have heard about. While grey lady ghosts are not uncommon – there are probably hundreds reported throughout the country – what makes the university ghost stand out is that she may in fact be a number of different spirits. There have been witness reports for years of encounters with the Grey Lady, but descriptions vary, with some describing her as a young woman, and others describing her as elderly. Descriptions of her clothing also vary between her wearing a Victorian style dress, right up to clothes similar to those that would have been worn in the mid-twentieth century. Whether this is a sign that she is the collective energy of a number of people associated with the university, or somehow has the ability to show herself as she would have been at various stages in her life, is unknown, and as her identity is also a mystery it is impossible to establish more details about her.

Sightings of the Grey Lady seem to occur more regularly at night, with security guards reporting seeing someone in the grounds yet when they go to investigate there is no one there. Others have had closer encounters, when they have seen the figure while out doing their rounds, only to find she vanishes as they approach. One of the earliest encounters appears to have been with one of the porters at the Pearce Lodge. He is reported to have seen an elderly lady dressed in grey approach the door of the lodge; yet when he opened it there were no signs of her. Quite distressed and confused at his encounter, the porter told his story to his colleagues and was reassured that he had simply seen the Grey Lady. Her form has also been seen standing staring at passers-by from one of the windows in the tower of the Pearce Lodge.

The Pearce Lodge itself has a somewhat unusual story. In 1870 some of the older buildings of the university were demolished, but an old entrance to Glasgow High Street was carefully dismantled with the stone being placed in storage. In 1887, when new campus buildings were being constructed at the Gilmorehill site, the preserved stonework was incorporated into the new entrance and gatehouse. While this allowed some of the architectural features of the original entrance to be included in the new building, quite why so much care was taken with this particular entrance is a bit of a mystery. It does, however, seem that the old stone may have brought something with it to the new gatehouse, with rumours spreading throughout the university that one of the rooms was haunted. Needless to say, a bet was soon placed within the student community, and one bold lad took up the challenge to spend the night locked in the haunted room. His bravery was soon to be tested, and it is said he had to be released shortly into his time having encountered books flying from the shelves and floating around the room.

Glasgow University. Author's collection

GLASGOW CALEDONIAN UNIVERSITY

Having been formed in 1993, Glasgow Caledonian University is a relatively new teaching establishment, although its history can be traced back to The Queen's College, which was founded in 1875. With modern campus buildings just a short walk from the city centre, the university is not a place you would immediately think was haunted, but there is something unusual happening in one of the lecture theatres, and I have first-hand experience of it as this was the university I attended.

Some of our studies were held in an underground lecture theatre, which was a particularly large room with no natural daylight, which gave it a dark and oppressive feeling. On a couple of occasions I thought I saw someone standing in the corner of the theatre, but every time I looked closely there was no one there. I shrugged it off as my mind playing games with me – it was after all one of the newest lecture theatres, and there would be no reason for it to be haunted. It was not until later in the term, when I overheard others talking about feeling uncomfortable while in that particular theatre, and seeing someone standing in the corner, that I started to wonder whether there was more to my own experiences.

I could still not rationalise why such a new building could be haunted, but I got my answer at the next lecture in that room. There was always an occasional 'rumble' while we were there, something not uncommon when underground and close to main roads. While attending an engineering lecture, our tutor paused until the rumble stopped before asking us if we knew what it was. He went on to explain that the theatre sits just a few metres above the Glasgow Underground, and he had been heavily involved in the design to ensure the tunnels were not damaged as part of the new build. As discussed earlier, the Glasgow Underground is home to several ghosts, as a result of houses being demolished to make way for the railway, deaths during construction and disturbed mass burials. This revelation raised the question of whether one of the spirits from the Underground or the lost villages could have found itself in the new, underground lecture theatre of the University. Unfortunately, it is a question I am never likely to be able to answer.

QUEEN'S PARK

Just four miles south of the city centre, you will find this impressive 150-acre park, surrounded by busy streets and Victorian buildings.

The area today gives no clue that this was a former battlefield, yet it was in this vicinity on 13 May 1568 that the Battle of Langside was fought. The opposing sides consisted of the forces of James Stewart, the Regent Moray, against the forces of his half-sister, Mary, Queen of Scots. Mary had been forced to abdicate the crown in favour of her infant son, and she was subsequently imprisoned, with James Stewart being appointed as the Regent to oversee the running of the country on behalf of his nephew, until such time as he was old enough to rule in his own right. Mary had, however, managed to escape and, as she still had a lot of supporters in the country who wanted to see her returned to the throne, she had been able to gather an army of around six thousand men to fight her cause.

They met with her brother's forces close to the village of Langside, which was then several miles south of Glasgow. As Mary's forces outnumbered her brothers by around two thousand men, the odds would appear to have been in Mary's favour. The commanders of the Regent Moray's forces, however, spotted a weak spot in Mary's defences, which they exploited, bringing the battle to an end within forty-five minutes. Only three hundred men were killed, a figure that would have been far higher if it had not been for the Regent Moray's decision to call off the pursuit of those fleeing.

The village of Langside soon became incorporated with the ever-growing city of Glasgow, and with the area becoming an established residential part of the city with parklands, and the battle long forgotten, it would be easy to imagine local residents' fears when they witnessed the ghostly figures of ancient soldiers marching close to the pond at Queen's Park on the anniversary of the battle. One woman was so terrified, she is said to have run to the local minister's house, who immediately came and prayed for the dead, releasing them from their attachment with the earth. Some say that this was successful and the soldiers have never been seen since, although others will tell you otherwise, and claim that the shadowy figures and sounds of the army from the last battle of Mary, Queen of Scots, still haunt this area.

Queen's Park. Author's collection

VICTORY BATHS, RENFREW

Just a few miles outside Glasgow, in the town of Renfrew, sits the Victory Baths, an Edwardian bath house built in 1921 to provide facilities for the local community. The building remains substantially unaltered, and has developed quite a reputation for being haunted.

With regular reports of unexplained noises and footsteps, the sound of whistling, light anomalies and items going missing or being moved, there are suggestions that there may be as many as nine or ten spirits that wander through the building. There are, however, just two that seem to be witnessed on a regular basis, and it is more likely that all of the phenomena are down to them. A young woman dressed in white has been seen throughout the building, including in an underground storage tunnel. The ghost is reported to appear to stare at those who see her, before vanishing, leaving staff feeling uneasy in certain areas of the building, with some refusing to go to those parts of the baths unaccompanied. Despite her being seen on a relatively regular basis, there is no information on who the lady in white is.

The ghost of a young boy has also been reported at the baths, and this is believed to be the spirit of a child who tragically lost his life in a diving accident at the pool around eighty years ago. This phantom has also been seen in various parts of the building, but there are some particularly frightening reports of encounters with this spirit, including small handprints appearing on the walls of the changing cubicles while they are being washed down. On another occasion, one of the cleaners was throwing scoops of water across the floor in preparation for cleaning it, when the form of a figure appeared in the water, although there was no one there. This poor soul seems to be lost, as some of those who have carried out paranormal investigations report that the spirit of the child follows them throughout the night, and so it is likely that he is trying to get attention and help, rather than to scare anyone.

Victory Baths, Renfrew. Thomas Nugent

HAUNTED PRISONS
BARLINNIE PRISON

In a suburb to the north-east of Glasgow city centre, lies Barlinnie Prison. The city originally had eight prisons, and the construction of Barlinnie, which opened in 1882, saw them gradually close as prisoners were transferred to the new facilities. Conditions in the prison were hard, with small, dark cells and, despite being extended several times to accommodate more prisoners, some cells did not have toilet facilities until as late as 2003.

Now Scotland's largest prison, Barlinnie has seen a long list of notorious criminals within its walls, some of whom never made it

Barlinnie Prison. Richard Webb

out. The execution of prisoners had previously been carried out at nearby Duke Street Prison, but the first execution in Barlinnie took place on 8th February 1946 by hanging. A total of ten prisoners were executed over the years, with the last taking place in 1960. All of those executed had been convicted of murder and their bodies were buried in unmarked graves within the prison grounds. With such a history, it would be fair to assume that the prison may be haunted by one or more of the prisoners who lost their life there, yet the ghost that is said to lurk within the prison grounds is in fact a woman. Her phantom, always seen wearing Victorian clothing and holding up an old fashioned lantern, walks silently through the grounds and into the former execution block. Her identity or her involvement at the execution block is not known, but one of the most interesting features of the haunting is her form walks through a door that was bricked up a long time ago.

Barlinnie is not the only haunted location connected to the former prisoners of Glasgow. In Cathedral Square, the Cathedral House Hotel can be found, a purpose built hostel that was constructed in 1877 to provide accommodation for newly released prisoners from Duke Street Prison. Now a modern hotel, there have been numerous reports of a ghost that brushes past guests as they climb the stairs. The spirit is not seen, yet those who have encountered it clearly feel as though someone is passing by close to them, yet no one is seen anywhere else on the staircase. The sound of children running around and laughing is also heard on the top floor, with the ghostly figures of two children being seen on several occasions, before vanishing. Paranormal investigations at the hotel have revealed a number of anomalies, including fluctuation with the electrics, furniture moving with no apparent cause and disembodied voices being recorded, perhaps those of the ghost on the stairs and the children.

In a private residence at an undisclosed address in Duke Street, the spirit of another inmate also is said to lurk. Numerous unexplained activity has occurred, such as the sound of footsteps and items moving but the most frightening encounter has been with a shadow figure, who approaches witnesses with its arms raised, before vanishing. Those who have seen it note that it is missing one hand, possibly the result of an incident during their time in the prison. A phantom dog is also said to roam the same property, mostly seem by children who happily play with it.

Duke Street Prison was demolished in 1958 and all that remains is part of the external wall. A housing development was constructed on the site between 1961 and 1964 and while the prison is long forgotten by many; one spirit from the prison remains in the form of a phantom woman seen walking through the area. She is normally accompanied by the sound of rattling keys, indicating she was one of the prison guards, who appears to still be patrolling to make sure the area is safe.

ABOUT THE AUTHOR

I have been interested in ghost stories and the unexplained since I was a child, having been introduced to the paranormal world by my grandfather, who was a specialist in fine gold leaf detailing and worked in many historical buildings.

Since then I have amassed a large collection of books and tales of hauntings from all over the world, and my investigative work has given me access to some of the most haunted locations in the country, ranging from historic buildings and secret undergrounds to seemingly ordinary family homes. I have heard and recorded disembodied voices, sometimes giving direct answers to questions, I have heard the slam of doors in a former prison where doors no longer exist, I have seen figures appear where they shouldn't be, before vanishing and I even own two 'haunted dolls', which have proven to be particularly active on occasion. Yet I remain an open-minded sceptic, which I believe to be essential

It has always fascinated me that so many people, who do not know each other, have similar experiences or see the same things in certain places, years or even centuries apart. It is easy to dismiss these occurrences, but less easy to offer an explanation. The truth for what causes these incidents is, quite definitely, out there, it just needs to be discovered.

More Ghost Stories for you to enjoy from
BRADWELL BOOKS

OUT NOW

Black Country & Birmingham Ghost Stories

Cambridgeshire Ghost Stories

Cheshire Ghost Stories

Cornish Ghost Stories

Cotswolds Ghost Stories

Cumbrian Ghost Stories

Derbyshire Ghost Stories

Dorset Ghost Stories

Essex Ghost Stories

Hampshire & the Isle of Wight Ghost Stories

Herefordshire Ghost Stories

Kent Ghost Stories

Lancashire Ghost Stories

Leicestershire Ghost Stories

London Ghost Stories

London Underground Ghost Stories

Norfolk Ghost Stories

North Wales Ghost Stories

Oxfordshire Ghost Stories

Scottish Ghost Stories

Shropshire Ghost Stories

Somerset& Bristol Ghost Stories

South Wales Ghost Stories

Staffordshire Ghost Stories

Surrey Ghost Stories

Sussex Ghost Stories

Warwickshire Ghost Stories

Welsh Celebrity Ghost Stories

Wiltshire Ghost Stories

Yorkshire Ghost Stories

OUT IN 2017

Nottinghamshire Ghost Stories

Lincolnshire Ghost Stories

**Buy on line from
Bradwell Books**

www.Bradwellbooks.co.uk